Observing Young Children

A Tool for Meaningful Assessment

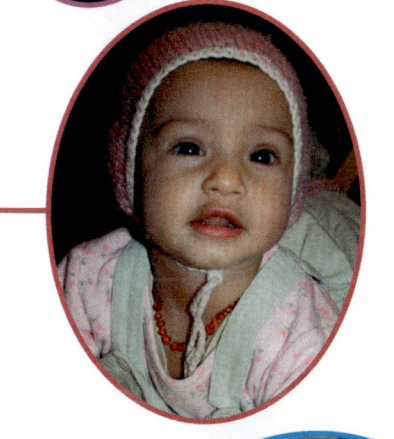

Observing Young Children

A Tool for Meaningful Assessment

AGES BIRTH TO FIVE

Mary O'Connell

Copyright © 2018 by Mary O'Connell

First Edition

ISBN-13: 978-1983894381

ISBN-10: 1983894389

Permission is granted to reproduce portions of this book for personal and educational use only. Commercial copying, hiring or lending is prohibited.

Book design and composition by Chelsea Cloeter
Cover photography by Bridget Schneider

To purchase a copy of this book, go to www.lifewaysnorthamerica.org.

ACKNOWLEDGEMENTS

With special thanks to my colleagues at LifeWays Early Childhood Center in Milwaukee, WI, who helped bring this tool into being, most especially Jaimmie Stugard, Jane Danner Sustar, and Emily Hall.

A huge thank you to Cynthia Aldinger and Rahima Baldwin Dancy for their editorial help and for inspiring so many of us involved in this work of caring for children. "Thank you" is truly insufficient for the debt of gratitude I personally owe to each of you, but it will have to do for now.

Thank you to Chelsea Cloeter for her beautiful design work and Ann Erwin for her professional and stylistic copy editing.

For sharing her beautiful photos of her children, most especially those of our "cover girl," thank you to Bridget Schneider, who lives and breathes the qualities of intention and simplicity as beautifully as anyone I know.

For the other photos of children gracing the pages of this book, many thanks to our wonderful LifeWays community of committed parents, caregivers and teachers who shared inspiring glimpses into your daily lives with children: Holly Haebig, Jenna Phillips, Ginger Fruncek, Lynn Coalson, Christine O'Connell, Bridget Minster, Laura Martin, Kristin Luce, Amber Brooks, Dorothy Kulke, Ona Wetherall, Bianca Amann and Rahel Kloppenburg.

CONTENTS

Introduction 9
How to Observe Children 13
How to Use the Developmental Timelines 17
Child Observation Recording Pages 19

The Timelines of Development (Ages Birth to 5 Years)

Typical Progression 21

SOCIAL/EMOTIONAL DEVELOPMENT

Connection and Autonomy 22
Rhythms and Routines 24
Self-Regulation Skills 26
Manners and Social Norms 27
Play 28
Empathy 30

PHYSICAL DEVELOPMENT

Manipulation of Objects 31
Sense of Balance 32
Mobility 34
Fine Motor Control 36
Stillness/Rest 38
Self-Help and Physical Needs 40
Limits and Boundaries 42
Use of Tools 43

COGNITIVE DEVELOPMENT

Spatial Awareness 44
Sorting and Arranging 45
Senses 46
Memory 48

Patterns and Rhythms 50
Awareness of Time 51
Following Directions and Processes 52
Numbers and Counting 53
Drawing (Curves and Lines) 54
Drawing (People and Houses) 56
Problem-Solving 58

LANGUAGE DEVELOPMENT

Non-Verbal Communication 59
Vocabulary and Syntax 60
Conversation 62
Expressive Language 63
Attending to and Comprehending Meaning from Books 64
Listening to and Understanding Oral Stories 65
Rhyming, Storytelling and Jokes 66
Letters, Sounds, Symbols and Writing 67

APPROACH TO LEARNING

The Child's Nature 69
Learning Style(s) 70
Culture 71

Conclusion 73
Research-based Tools and Other Resources 75
Endnotes 77

INTRODUCTION

Moments after the birth of my daughter, our third child, she looked up at me with her dark, slate-colored eyes and stared into my eyes very intently. It felt as though she looked right through me and into my very soul. It was disarming, to say the least. I'd already given birth to our two sons but, in the sterile, stark hospital environment surrounding their births, if this intense gaze had occurred, I had completely missed it. My daughter's birth, in the same hospital, was quieter and more intentional – not through my intentions, mind you. I had yet to learn that birth without fear or medical intervention was a possibility, and my husband was happy to have me take the lead in decisions about such things as birthing. So here we were, back at the hospital for our third birth, and, as luck or fate would have it, a March snowstorm delayed the doctor's arrival. In her absence, the doctor directed the nursing staff to call the hospital's midwifery clinic to see if there was a nurse-midwife available to attend the birth. As soon as our nurse-midwife entered the room, it was as if a guardian angel had descended. Lights lowered, her soft voice and calm presence permeated the room and created an environment in which there was no fear, no rushing. The mood was of peaceful anticipation and expectant joy. There were many gifts offered to us by this angel/midwife, and one of them was that I was able to be present for "the gaze" of this fresh-from-heaven soul in the moments after her birth.

It lasted for just a fleeting moment in time—only a few seconds—but something about the way this tiny, minutes-old babe met my eye felt eternal, as if she had arrived from a time and place that was beyond my understanding. She seemed to possess a "knowing" that accompanied her from whence she came. After the moment passed, in my arms was a beautiful, typical newborn, unfocused, sometimes calm and sometimes fussy, the apple of her parents' eyes. I would not encounter the gaze again, but I will never forget it.

In her book, *Life Is the Curriculum,* Cynthia Aldinger describes the experience as one that is more universal than what I knew at the time:

> *Have you ever been caught in the gaze of an infant and had the feeling that someone with depth and breadth, character and clarity, knowledge and wonderings was staring at you? It may have been only for a brief moment, but you felt a quickening in your soul, didn't you? "Who are you?" you may have wanted to say. But the answer to that question is not really what matters. What matters is whether or not you are willing to entertain the thought that this fresh, innocent one in your arms is already Some One. And it is no accident that she or he is in your arms at that moment and has come to learn from and teach you in the Vast Unfolding.*

Perhaps you have experienced moments such as this with your own child, or with a child in your care, in which you have sensed the child has arrived here on Earth with his or her own individuality, a past, present and future that seems to transcend both nature and nurture and seems more related to destiny.

Along with this eternal "law of individuality," we also observe that each growing child has a unique development and biography. Development throughout childhood is complex. While the timelines of development that follow in this book may appear straightforward, child development is neither simply incremental nor linear. Throughout the early years of childhood there are developmental patterns: bodily abilities that morph and grow into other abilities, a growing brain that develops new capacities while pruning others, and the ever changing social/emotional needs of the child. Besides the child's emerging individual temperament, there are also temperamental tendencies that accompany each age. We're familiar with the secure toddler who becomes anxious and inconsolable as the result of separation anxiety when his mother steps away, and we know this, too, shall pass. We understand that the obstinate two-and-a-half year old whose favorite word is "No!" will not stay this contrary forever. We realize, hopefully, that the five-year-old who shouts at her good friend, "You aren't invited to my birthday party!" is not developing into a drama queen; she is simply learning to manage the emotions that accompany social interactions at this age.

"Salutogenesis" is a term coined by Aaron Antonovsky, a professor of medical sociology, to describe an approach to care that focuses on the factors that support human health and well-being rather than on the factors that cause illness and disease. We can apply this concept of salutogenesis to inform our observation of children by beginning with the recognition that each person is a unique spiritual being on a human journey that is his or hers alone. This journey requires a particular constellation of capacities, challenges and experiences, and these are not necessarily "good" or "bad," "normal" or "abnormal." They are simply the capacities, challenges and experiences needed to fulfill his or her destiny. When we take the time to observe, we are able to develop a fuller picture of the child without attaching our own judgments or hoped-for outcomes, and we are able to meet the child with the support he or she needs on this journey. This allows us to respect the inevitable peaks and valleys that accompany growth and development while providing an environment that allows the child to develop as healthily as possible. Through the simple practice of observation, we can lay the foundation of care that is truly worthy of our children.

Many of the early childhood observation and assessment systems on the market today are focused on assessing skills and evaluating whether a child has the "right" number of skills for someone his age. Frankly, I have felt pretty allergic to these assessment systems for many years. If we truly believe that every child has come for a reason, with intention and purpose, and if we trust in the wisdom of his or her destiny, it seems pretty presumptuous to assess the child's development with a chart or a checklist, doesn't it? And yet, there have been times over the years when a system of observing and documenting children's development has been asked for. Parents seek reassurance that their child is developing within the typical spectrum of development, and they ask for ways in which they can support their child's next steps. Caregivers and teachers wonder how to identify developmental challenges in children so they can offer the best support to the child and well-researched information to the parents. Childcare quality ratings systems have been implemented in almost every state in the U.S., and most (if not all) of them require that, to receive public funds, an early childhood program must have a system of child observation and assessment in place. Over time, I began to see the value in an observation and assessment tool that honors the child as an individual while also giving a picture of archetypal child development.

When LifeWays Early Childhood Center in Milwaukee, where I worked as the director, was faced with receiving a lower rating in Wisconsin's Youngstar quality rating system (QRS) unless we adopted a system of observation and assessment, our QRS representative encouraged our staff to create one that honored our view of the developing child. The observation practices and developmental timelines that follow in this book are the result of that process. The child observation suggestions are largely inspired by the Integration of Learning Requirements for students in the LifeWays Early Childhood Certification Training, as well as some helpful guidance regarding child study from the wider community of Waldorf educators. The need for a system of assessment that was research-based and acceptable to the ratings systems people led to the creation of the developmental timelines, which came about from my colleagues and I asking ourselves the question, "What skills and capacities do we want to help children develop at LifeWays?" Our answers to this question helped us to create a list of research-based areas of development, categorized within the five developmental domains recognized by the Wisconsin Model Early Learning Standards: Social/Emotional, Physical, Cognitive, Language, and Approach to Learning. After we implemented this process for a couple of years, it was accepted by the state of Wisconsin for use in our center.

We hope you will find this tool useful. You might decide to develop a practice of observation and journaling, creating a simple portfolio for each child in your care. If you find yourself in a situation that requires you to have a system of observation and assessment, perhaps you can apply to have this tool approved by your state or quality rating system. Maybe you just want a research-based tool to reference during parent conferences, or to have on hand when you have questions about the development of the children in your care. The ways you use this tool are completely up to you.

HOW TO OBSERVE CHILDREN

How do we do observe the child in a way that reveals to us the true nature of the child and not simply a problem to be solved? Here, as in many areas, I am grateful for the work of Rudolf Steiner, the founder of Waldorf education.

Steiner had a very particular way of observing children. In Peter Selg's book, *The Therapeutic Eye,* Selg describes how Steiner approached children with sincere, warm interest. In his curative education course, Steiner told teachers to develop *loving devotion which creates the ability in you simply to look at the things which matter.* I don't think he was referring to how many letters the child recognizes or whether he can count to 100. The young child "thinks" with his body. How he uses his body to move and interact with the world is our greatest teacher when we are observing the child before the age of seven, and his actions tell us much about who he is and how he is experiencing life.

We know the ways in which we interact with children make a difference in their self-esteem and how they view their own capacities. The ways in which we observe children make a difference as well, not only in the way we view them, but also in the way we respond to them based on our observations. All of this ultimately affects the way the child sees himself or herself. It is our professional responsibility as teachers and caregivers to make a habit of observing not just those children we are concerned about, but every child in our care. Our observations are the result of a process that begins with sincere, warm interest in the child, with examining our own behavior in relationship to the child and then sharing our observations with colleagues or partners who add their own observations and insights to the conversation. We do this observation to educate ourselves about the individual child as well as archetypal child development. As we sharpen our observation skills as teachers and caregivers, we are transformed in the process. Our goal should not be to change the child, but to open ourselves to a true picture of the child so we can offer him or her the care that best supports his or her health and wellbeing.

First Observations

When a child first comes into our care, we may observe him physically. Is the child long and lean or more compact and muscular? Fair or dark? Small-headed or large-headed? Does he tend to be cool or warm? These are all ways to begin to know the child.

Then we begin to observe and record the following:

How does the child move?
How does the child speak?
How does he or she listen?
How does the child play?
How does he or she interact with others?
How does the child eat?
How does the child sleep and wake?

When observing these things and recording our observations, it is important to be objective. This is simple, but not at all easy! In our LifeWays Early Childhood Certification Training, to hone their objective observation skills, students practice observing two children over the course of months. They learn to record an observation as, "Timmy eats all of his bread and leaves his vegetables on the plate," in contrast to, "Timmy likes bread, but he dislikes vegetables." If we allow our observations to be subjective, we are simply reinforcing our own biases and feelings about the child. When we learn the art of objective observation, we can begin to trust our observations to teach us about the child.

Some caregivers choose to keep a small notebook in their apron pocket and jot down observations throughout the day. Others choose to write down observations at nap time or other times when they are not in the presence of the children. It's up to you to determine how best to record what you see with the least disruption and the most accuracy and objectivity. At first it can seem daunting and time-consuming, but I recommend developing a regular practice of jotting down a word or two as you observe something, then going back later and writing the full observation in your journal. You will soon have a treasured collection of observational records to share with parents and to inform your own caregiving or teaching. At LifeWays Milwaukee, each primary caregiver has two hours of scheduled time per week when they are not with the children to devote to this journaling.

Another way to gain information about the child is to have a conversation with his or her parents. The ways in which children act and react at home can be very different than the way they do in your program. Do not forget your colleagues. If you work in a school or center setting, your co-workers will be able to offer their observations, and these can often be more objective than your own because they are a little further removed from the day-to-day care of the child.

After taking some time to gather these observations, it's a good practice to take the full picture that you have developed of the child into your sleep. According to Laurie Clark in her article, "A Contemplative and Reflective Format for Early Childhood Study" (*Gateways,* Waldorf Early Association of North America), this allows us to "let go of the information that has been gathered about the child, stop thinking about it, and open toward the echo that lives out in the world of sleep. ... There is a gesture from the teacher of attentive listening upon meeting the child, with an awareness and hope that the angel of the child may reveal a picture as a seed planted. Impressions and inspirations that arise out of sleep then may be a flowering of this seed that can be received as a kind of heart offering laid out for the child." Even if the idea of the child's angel doesn't resonate with you, taking an image of the child into your sleep is still a valid practice, if only to allow your subconscious mind to help you develop an understanding that your conscious mind may not be able to. Perhaps this image of the child's guardian angel revealing a picture to you is quite meaningful. I have found it to be true over my twenty-some years of working with children, and it has become a valuable practice for me.

Only after a period of comprehensive observation and reflection do we pick up the developmental profile timelines on the pages that follow. There are many intangible qualities of young children that cannot be captured on the timelines. A child's personality, persistence, health, confidence and other soul qualities cannot be charted. This developmental timeline charting is really helpful only after we have gotten to know the child.

HOW TO USE THE DEVELOPMENTAL TIMELINES

The intended way to use the developmental timelines is to observe the child as she naturally moves through her day. The blank spaces next to each developmental step are for you to record the date on which you observed the behavior. There are also blank lines on each page to record your notes about what you observed. Some caregivers try to do a complete observation of each child every three months or so, going through each timeline and noting which steps reflect the child's current stage of development. Others find that a more organic, sporadic way of charting works better for them. Of course, if you are using these timelines to meet the criteria of a rating system or accreditation organization, you'll need to follow their requirements.

The way you should *not* use these charts is to set up a scenario to "test" whether or not a child can do a particular skill. For example, please do not sit a child down and ask him to draw a circle to see if he can do it. If you see a child draw a circle when he is working with his crayons, make a note of the date you observed it. This means you may not observe or document every single action on these timelines. So be it. It is far more important to get to know the individual child as he or she unfolds than to measure or record.

How are these developmental timelines useful?
- They help us see where a child is in his or her development and what to expect next, so we can provide the best environment possible. For example, if we observe that the child is in a phase of negativism and we see that a stage of more cooperative behavior generally follows, we may decide to hold off on toilet training until the child is a bit more agreeable. (Social/Emotional: Connection and Autonomy)

- They help us to notice trends across the domains of development, to see where a child may need a bit more support. For example, a child may exhibit early development in the realm of physical development but may be showing slower development in the realm of language. Often this just tells us a bit about who he is. We may be encouraged to support his language development with the use of stories, nursery rhymes or songs.

- They offer a tool to use when discussing a child's development with his or her parents. Because these timelines are research-based, they can indicate for parents where their child lands on the scales of typical development. This can be a relief or a cause for concern, depending on the situation. Please remember that you are not a diagnostician. Your sincere, warm interest and personal observations will go a long way in helping parents accompany the child on his or her journey. If you have concerns about a child's development you should encourage the parent to talk to others with more specialized expertise, such as the child's pediatrician.

- Sometimes the school a child will be transitioning to requests a report about the child, and this packet of developmental profiles with your observations recorded over a period of time can be useful (with permission from the child's parents to release it, of course.)

- It can be part of a file given to parents when a child "graduates" from your program, as a record of just how far the child has come, along with your personal written observations. This file can also include drawings or paintings the child created or photographs you have taken.

(You will see on the developmental timelines that follow there are blank spaces for recording notes. You may simply copy the pages of this book to keep observational records for multiple children. There is also an inexpensive PDF file available for purchase on the LifeWays North America website that includes more space for recording notes, and allows you to easily print out as many copies as you need or use the fillable fields to keep all of your records electronically.)

CHILD OBSERVATION

First, observe the child physically. Record your physical observations here:

_____
_____
_____
_____
_____
_____

Next, record observations of the following behaviors as objectively as possible:

How does the child move?

_____
_____
_____
_____

How does the child speak?

_____
_____
_____
_____

How does the child listen?

How does the child play?

How does the child interact with others?

How does the child eat?

How does the child sleep and wake?

THE TIMELINES OF DEVELOPMENT (Ages Birth to 5 Years)

- Infant to six months
- Six months to twelve months
- Age 1
- Age 1½
- Age 2
- Age 3
- Age 4
- Age 5

Typical Progression

Although the developmental timelines that follow were created using the age progression listed here, the timelines themselves do not indicate ages. This is intentional, for each child progresses in his own way at his own pace. By not having ages next to each developmental stage, we can pay attention to where the child is and where he is going rather than concerning ourselves with whether or not he is "on time." The range of typical development is very broad, and age-based charts often tempt us to do all sorts of unhealthy comparing of children.

When it came time to create a system that would pass muster with the state's rating system folks, however, a listing of ages and stages was expected as is common for these types of tools. Indicating the age progression on this page is our way of compromising to meet this expectation.

Although we know there is no such thing as a "typical" child, there are some archetypal patterns in development. If you want to look at what is typical development for an average two-year old, for example, you will see that the two-year old is represented here in the fifth stage of development. You can go through the timelines (exceptions are noted) and look at every fifth entry. This will give you a profile of the typical two-year old child.

SOCIAL/EMOTIONAL: Connection and Autonomy

_____ Recognition
- Recognizes and reaches out to familiar faces
- Stops crying when caregiver approaches

_____ Preference
- Distinguishes among and responds differently to strangers
- Begins to show preference for primary caregiver

_____ Anxiety
- Exhibits fear of strangers (stranger anxiety)
- Resists separating from familiar adult (separation anxiety)

_____ Emerging self
- Remains friendly toward others
- Recognizes self in mirror
- Begins to assert independence

_____ Contrariness
- Orders adults around
- Makes demands and expects immediate compliance
- May display extreme negativism toward adult

_____ Cooperation
- Strives for independence, yet needs reassurance that caregiver is available
- More peaceful and cooperative with adults

Growing independence

- Shows pride in accomplishments
- Seeks frequent adult approval
- Shows growing need for independence

Competency

- Continues to need adult reassurance, but may be less open to seeking or accepting comfort from adult
- Boasts about accomplishments

Relationship-based care with consistent adults is essential for infants to develop trust.

SOCIAL/EMOTIONAL DEVELOPMENT 23

SOCIAL/EMOTIONAL: Rhythms and Routines

_____ Recognition
- Recognizes and enjoys familiar routines, such as diaper changes
- Sleeping/waking may not be rhythmic

_____ Sleep and food
- More rhythmic in eating and sleeping
- Begins to participate in family's or program's meal routines

_____ Adjusting
- May struggle with sleep rhythms when adjusting from frequent shorter naps to fewer long naps each day
- Tantrums may result when overly tired due to changing sleep rhythms

_____ Conflict during routines
- Consistently follows schedule of meals and naps
- Often refuses to cooperate with daily routines that were once stress-free (such as dressing, putting on shoes)

_____ Internalizing rhythm
- Steady rhythm helps to avoid conflicts during transitions
- Usually complies with expectations if given ample warning

_____ Relying on rhythm
- Changes in routine prompt many questions ("What are you doing?" "Where are we going?")

Planning around rhythm

- Begins to plan ahead ("After snack, can we go to the park?")
- Understands rhythm ("Is today Soup Day?")
- Explains rhythm to others

Rhythm as it relates to time

- Begins to relate clock time to the daily schedule ("I wake up at 6 o'clock.")
- Begins to understand what a calendar is for

Involving the young child in the regular routines of meal preparation encourages her to try new foods.

SOCIAL/EMOTIONAL DEVELOPMENT

SOCIAL/EMOTIONAL: Self-Regulation Skills[1]

_____ ### Regulates response
- Sucks thumb, looks away or otherwise calms self when environment becomes over-stimulating

_____ ### Calms self
- Can routinely self-calm except when ill or in unfamiliar surroundings

_____ ### Curious
- Shows exceeding curiosity about people or surroundings
- Can get into unsafe situations easily without adult guidance

_____ ### Inhibits responses
- Demonstrates the ability to inhibit impulses at caregiver's request ("Come here now so I can put on your shoes.")

_____ ### Cues lead to self-regulation
- Translates cues from the adult ("Your turn is next") into regulation that helps inhibit urges

_____ ### Co-regulates with adults
- Takes turns when reminded
- Joins in group activities but may need help to do so
- Plays nicely with others, yet can become aggressive at times

_____ ### Refinement
- Demonstrates an understanding that clapping, talking or being noisy is appropriate at certain times but not at others

_____ ### Internalized self-regulation
- Attends to and recognizes situations that offer potential for interesting interactions or learning
- Persists in challenging activities

An essential task for the preschool-aged child is learning to live with others in community.

SOCIAL/EMOTIONAL: Manners and Social Norms

_____ ### Responds
- Smiles in response to a friendly face or voice

_____ ### Imitates sounds
- Imitates sounds others make

_____ ### Imitates actions
- Enjoys others' attention and imitates actions

_____ ### Helps
- Enjoys helping with chores, such as cleaning up

_____ ### Emerging table manners
- Learns table manners by imitating adults and other children
- Finds it difficult to wait to be served

_____ ### Social interaction rituals
- Joins in social interaction rituals, such as "Hi," "Bye," "Please"
- Promotes others' behavior: "You go first"

_____ ### Enjoys socializing
- Talking takes precedence over eating
- Tests limits with potty talk
- Tattles on others

_____ ### Entertains
- Likes to entertain people and make them laugh
- Knows the "right" way to do things and can be opinionated

Using real plates, bowls, cups and utensils helps the young child learn table manners.

SOCIAL/EMOTIONAL DEVELOPMENT

SOCIAL/EMOTIONAL: Play [2]

_____ Unoccupied play
- Seemingly random movements lead to purposeful movements

_____ Solitary play
- Enjoys putting things on head
- Puts things in and out of each other
- Throws toys on the floor and expects adult to retrieve them

_____ Onlooker play
- Mouths toys less often
- Imitates others' actions
- Enjoys companionship of other children, yet plays alone

_____ Parallel play
- Strong sense of property rights ("MINE!")
- Plays alongside other children, but not with other children

_____ Symbolic play
- Pretending with toys that look like real life objects (pretending to eat play food, making animals walk)

_____ Associative play
- Plays with other children in loosely structured activities
- Often will still play parallel to others
- Uses objects symbolically (a block can now be a car)

_____ Emerging cooperative play
- Participates in group activities
- Wants to be with other children
- Begins to have a best friend

Secure cooperative play

- Organizes and communicates with other children as they work toward a common goal
- Suggests imaginative and elaborate ideas

Plenty of time for creative, free play offers the child many benefits, including the opportunity to develop friendships.

SOCIAL/EMOTIONAL DEVELOPMENT 29

SOCIAL/EMOTIONAL: Empathy

_____ ## Responsive
- Responds differently to facial expressions (frowns, smiles)

_____ ## Sociable
- Looks for ways to win the approval and attention of others

_____ ## Egocentric
- Demonstrates a belief that everyone and everything exists for child's own benefit
- Grabs things and people

_____ ## Curious about others
- Still primarily egocentric, yet shows increasing curiosity about others' emotions

_____ ## Caring
- Shows signs of empathy
- Sometimes overzealous with hugs

_____ ## Affectionate
- Shows affection towards children who are younger
- Empathetic to child who is hurt

_____ ## Contradictory
- Generally caring of others, yet often may appear to be selfish
- May use name-calling and taunting to exclude others

_____ ## Generous
- Is often quite generous
- Affectionate and caring, especially toward animals
- Can be protective of younger sibling

Spending time in nature allows the child to develop empathy for even the slimiest slugs.

30 OBSERVING YOUNG CHILDREN

PHYSICAL: Manipulation of Objects

_____ Hands
- Tugs and pulls on own hands

_____ Reach
- Reaches for objects
- Grasps and releases objects

_____ Transfer
- Transfers objects from one hand to another

_____ Play
- Plays with objects

_____ Stiff movements
- Picks up and throws objects
- Kicks objects with stiff movements

_____ Fluid movements
- Manipulates items with flexible body movements
- Carries objects easily

_____ Coordination
- Pedals
- Kicks a ball by running up to it
- Catches a ball with arms extended

_____ Full range of motion
- Uses full range of motion
- Throws with distance and aim
- Catches a ball thrown from three feet away

High quality rain gear allows the toddler to scoop and pour to her heart's content.

PHYSICAL DEVELOPMENT 31

PHYSICAL: Sense of Balance

_____ ### Reflex
- Exhibits Moro (startle) reflex[3]
- Coordinates vocalizing, looking and movements

_____ ### Depth perception
- Shows fear of falling off high places, such as changing table or stairs

_____ ### Sitting
- Sits unaided
- Shifts positions without falling
- Stands with assistance

_____ ### Standing
- Stands without assistance
- Kneels while playing
- Gets into and out of chair
- Squats and stands with ease

_____ ### Balance while moving
- Jumps but may fall down
- Throws a large ball underhand without losing balance

_____ ### Refining balance
- Balances momentarily on one foot
- Jumps in place
- Kicks a ball without falling

Sustaining balance

- Sustains balance during movement (e.g., climbing trees or equipment, walking along the edge of a low wall)

Secure balance

- Walks on a beam
- Hops on one foot
- Attempts to jump rope

It is important to allow the child to come to a standing position on his own, unaided by bouncers, activity seats or other devices.

PHYSICAL: Mobility

_____ **Rolls**
- Moves to explore
- Rolls over

_____ **Scoots**
- Scoots backward or forward

_____ **Creeps/crawls**
- Creeps
- Crawls
- Pulls to stand
- Cruises furniture while holding on

_____ **Walks**
- Walks unassisted
- Experiments with different ways of moving

_____ **Refines walking**
- Experiments with speed of walking and moving
- Marches

_____ **Climbs and jumps**
- Climbs stairs (not alternate feet)
- Jumps off low step

_____ **Moves fluidly**
- Runs
- Starts and stops
- Moves around obstacles
- Jumps over small objects

Moves with coordination
- Climbs up and down stairs (alternate feet)
- Skips
- Gallops
- Spins

Simple, natural structures and logs allow the child to practice climbing at his own pace.

PHYSICAL: Fine Motor Control

_____ Reaching
- Reflexive grip
- Reaches for objects with both arms simultaneously

_____ Refined reaching
- Reaches for objects with one hand or the other
- Reaches, grasps and puts objects in mouth

_____ Using fingers
- Explores new objects by poking with one finger
- Uses pincer grasp to pick up small objects

_____ Using two hands
- Uses one hand to hold object and the other hand to manipulate another object (e.g., holds cup and bangs spoon)
- Turns pages of book two or three at a time

_____ Pouring/filling
- Pours and fills sand and water
- Begins to stack four to six items

_____ Refining fine motor
- Builds with 8+ blocks
- Carries small pitcher without spilling
- Turns pages of book one at a time
- Washes dishes

Refined fine motor
- Forms shapes from dough or clay
- Threads beads on a string
- Uses non-dominant hand to assist and stabilize

Fine motor coordination
- Hand dominance well established
- Finger knits
- Can do simple sewing

Bits of finger foods on the tray help the infant refine her pincer grasp.

PHYSICAL: Stillness/Rest [4]

_____ ### Sleeps most of the time
- Sleeps 14–19 hours per day
- Likes to be held when awake

_____ ### Spends more time awake
- Takes two to three naps per day
- Active when awake

_____ ### Nap rhythm established
- Takes one to two naps per day
- Active when awake

_____ ### One daytime nap
- Takes one nap per day
- Active when awake

_____ ### Moments of stillness when awake
- Averages 12–14 hours of sleep, with one long nap during the day
- Stares for long moments when awake (e.g., Where did the ball go? What caused a noise?)
- Can sit for a short book

_____ ### Ten minutes stillness when awake
- Averages 12 hours of sleep; may give up nap at home
- Can sit still for a short oral story or a ten-minute book

_____ ### Mealtime stillness
- Averages 10–12 hours of sleep at night, depending upon nap
- Can sit at the table for mealtime without many reminders

15–20 minute stillness

- Averages 10–11 hours of sleep at night, depending upon nap
- Difficulty going to sleep if excited
- Can engage in 15–20 minute "still activity," such as listening to a story or painting

The forest or other natural setting allows the child to experience stillness.

PHYSICAL DEVELOPMENT

PHYSICAL: Self-Help and Physical Needs

_____ Dependent
- Cries to communicate needs
- Needs little assistance getting nipple to mouth
- May fuss when diaper needs changing

_____ Begins to help
- Reaches for cup and spoon while being fed
- Pulls off own socks
- May pull off wet diaper

_____ Understanding
- Understands use of objects such as comb or toothbrush
- Cooperates to a degree in being dressed
- May let adult know when diaper is soiled

_____ Emerging independence
- Uses spoon with some degree of skill
- Good control of cup
- Helps with dressing
- May let caregiver know when diaper is soiled or wet

_____ Increasing independence
- Feeds self with increasing skill
- Can usually undress self
- May show signs of readiness for toilet training

_____ Independent in group setting
- Uses spoon in semi-adult fashion
- Pours drinks
- Takes care of own toilet and handwashing needs
- Capable of dressing for outdoors

Helpful and independent

- Skilled at spreading butter and cutting soft foods
- Helps set the table
- Dresses self
- Folds laundry
- Puts clothes away

Ready for school

- Makes a simple meal (prepares cereal with milk or simple sandwich)
- Dresses self completely
- Learns to tie
- Uses tissue for blowing nose

The very young child wants to cooperate in dressing himself.

PHYSICAL DEVELOPMENT 41

PHYSICAL: Limits and Boundaries

_____ *Totally dependent*
- No sense of boundaries
- Dependent on the adult for safety

_____ *Needs adult presence*
- Can roll off surfaces if unattended

_____ *Needs adult vigilance*
- Gates and child safety locks are needed for safety

_____ *Responds to adult*
- Falls often
- Responds to "no" but may not always stop

_____ *Discovers cause and effect*
- Curious and active
- Motor skills outpace judgment
- Shows discovery of cause and effect

_____ *Follows directions*
- Abides by caregiver's directions most of the time
- Can go for walks at the child's pace

_____ *Practices self-confidence*
- Likes to test limits and practice self-confidence
- Abides by safety rules most of the time

_____ *Skill mastery*
- Quest for mastery of skills
- Self-confident and reliable
- Eagerness often interferes with ability to foresee danger

Testing the limits of her ability is an innate drive in the young child.

PHYSICAL: Use of Tools

_____ *Grasps items*
- Grasps with entire hand

_____ *Holds to mouth*
- Holds own bottle or pacifier

_____ *Learns to use cup*
- Begins to drink from cup
- Holds cup with two hands

_____ *Feeds self*
- Feeds self (needs help)
- Holds spoon

_____ *Grasps objects with one hand*
- Holds crayon with fist
- Grasps cup in one hand

_____ *Uses practical tools capably*
- Feeds self with minimal assistance
- Manipulates large buttons and zippers

_____ *Purposefully uses tools*
- Holds a crayon with a tripod grasp
- Paints or draws with purpose (may have an idea in mind but has trouble implementing)

_____ *Uses tools with control*
- Cuts on a line with scissors
- Reproduces shapes and maybe symbols
- Demonstrates fair control of crayon or pencil

It is wonderful when children are allowed to use real hand tools!

PHYSICAL DEVELOPMENT 43

COGNITIVE: Spatial Awareness

_____ ### Bodily experience
- Looks for or reaches toward objects that touch body

_____ ### Beginning object permanence
- Looks for or reaches toward objects that fall from view

_____ ### Object permanence
- Searches for objects moved from view

_____ ### Negotiates barriers
- Reaches object from behind a barrier
- Moves self around a barrier to get a desired object

_____ ### Daily routines
- Climbs up onto stool to reach sink for daily dish washing or teeth brushing
- Looks on specific shelves for desired toys
- Hides under a blanket

_____ ### Understands position
- Understands up, down, top, bottom, under, over, next to, beside

_____ ### Location spatial awareness
- Identifies landmarks (e.g., "It's by Grandma's house.")
- Objects when someone is in his/her personal space
- Understands backward and forward

_____ ### Developed spatial awareness
- Can "line up at the gate"
- Uses positional words in speech, such as in/out, front/back, next to, between
- Aware of others' space

_____
_____
_____
_____
_____
_____
_____

The toddler loves to experiment with spatial awareness by repeatedly stepping up and down a small step.

44 OBSERVING YOUNG CHILDREN

COGNITIVE: Sorting and Arranging

_____ *Differentiates*
- Differentiates between people and objects

_____ *Stacks and nests*
- Stacks objects
- Puts objects inside one another

_____ *Understands functions*
- Demonstrates understanding of functional relationships (puts spoon in bowl and pretends to eat)

_____ *Spatial and form discrimination*
- Puts all pegs in pegboard
- Puts all blocks in block cart

_____ *Classifies based on one dimension*
- Separates all toy cars from all toy animals

_____ *Sorts logically*
- Sorts objects logically based on one dimension (color or size)
- Compares sizes of items
- May explain to adult

_____ *Stacks graduated items*
- Builds pyramids with largest item on bottom
- Understands concepts of tallest, biggest, same and more

_____ *Examines and orders objects*
- Places objects in order (shortest to tallest; smallest to biggest; first, second, last)
- Understands concept of "half"
- Compares collected objects

_____
_____
_____
_____
_____
_____
_____
_____
_____
_____

The young child doesn't need many or varied sets of manipulatives to practice sorting!

COGNITIVE DEVELOPMENT 45

COGNITIVE: Senses [5]

_____ Related to self and primary caregiver
- Focuses eyes on objects
- Reacts to noises
- Prefers breast milk/formula
- Enjoys being cuddled
- Sense of smell highly developed (mother's scent can calm)

_____ Immediate surroundings
- Focuses at a distance
- Babbles to hear own voice
- Chooses what s/he touches
- Interested in tasting food

_____ Sight and hearing strengthened
- Near normal visual acuity
- Begins to use sight or hearing more than smell to differentiate objects/people

_____ Sensing and Interacting
- Choosier about taste – goes on food jags
- Can hear and respond (e.g., "Where is your nose?")
- Uses touch to show frustrations (hits, pushes, pulls hair)

_____ Exploring through senses
- Notices visual details – depth perception
- Likes simple, recognizable foods
- Explores everything in the environment

_____ Refining sensory input
- Resents being bothered when trying to listen to a story
- May continue to have a comfort object to nurture sense of touch

46 OBSERVING YOUNG CHILDREN

_____ *Responding to sensory input*
- Responds to statements without constant repeating
- Answers appropriately when asked what to do if tired, cold, hungry

_____ *Sensory readiness for classroom setting*
- Visual tracking and convergence developed (both eyes work together and focus on an object together)
- Often adopts food dislikes of others
- Speaks in a moderate voice

Time and space to be fully immersed in the natural world provides a wealth of rich sensory impressions.

COGNITIVE: Memory

_____ Localized memory
- Recognizes and reaches out to familiar faces and objects
- Turns toward familiar voices

_____ Object permanence
- Drops objects intentionally and looks for them

_____ Familiarity
- Locates familiar objects upon request
- Points to familiar people, animals and toys when asked

_____ Beginning rhythmic memory
- Enjoys repetitive stories
- Names objects that are repeatedly used

_____ Absence of the familiar
- Knows where familiar people should be and notes their absence
- Looks for people who aren't there and asks about them

_____ Acquired rhythmic memory
- Recites nursery rhymes
- Sings songs

_____ Picture memory
- Can form a mental picture and talk about people, events or activities that are not present

Developed memory

- States the name of own city or town
- Knows own birthday
- Tells parents' names
- Remembers jokes but may not re-tell them correctly
- Remembers holidays/festivals from last year

The infant develops memory by learning that consistent, caring adults will always be there when she needs them.

COGNITIVE: Patterns and Rhythms

_____ ### Familiar routines
- Recognizes familiar routines
- Begins rhythmic feeding, sleeping and bowel times

_____ ### Rhythmic activities
- Likes being gently, rhythmically swayed or bounced
- Vocalizes and dances to music

_____ ### Rhymes and songs
- Enjoys rhymes and songs
- Tries to join in

_____ ### Repetitive picture stories
- Enjoys being read picture stories with repetition

_____ ### Ritualistic
- Wants everything "just so"
- Expects routines to be carried out exactly as usual
- Spontaneously rhymes/chants

_____ ### Repetitive oral stories
- Recites nursery rhymes
- Sings songs
- Enjoys hearing repetitive stories

_____ ### Cues to signal routines
- Responds well to cues that signal routines (e.g., the mealtime blessing or cleanup song)

_____ ### Independent routines
- Carries out routine chores and can help younger children with routines
- Re-tells repetitive stories

The young child naturally begins to notice and play with patterns.

COGNITIVE: Awareness of Time

_____ ### Individualized
- Needs individualized feeding, sleeping and playing schedule

_____ ### Predictable pattern
- Begins a predictable pattern of feeding, sleeping and waking

_____ ### Meshes with family or group
- Needs begin to mesh with the needs of the group (sleep, food, play)

_____ ### Follows group routines
- Follows the daily routines of the group
- Still needs plenty of time to transition from one activity to the next

_____ ### Relies on routine
- Relies on daily routines to understand the passage of time ("Mommy will be here at lunchtime.")

_____ ### Understands duration of time
- Begins to understand the duration of time
- Says things like "all the time" and "the next day"
- Still confuses "yesterday" and "tomorrow"

_____ ### Sequences
- Understands and relates the sequence of daily events ("I get up, have breakfast and brush my teeth.")

_____ ### Begins to understand time
- Relates clock time to daily schedule ("I go to bed at 7 o'clock.")
- Knows what a calendar is for

Enjoying verses, songs and finger plays at a designated time each day helps children develop an awareness of time.

COGNITIVE DEVELOPMENT 51

COGNITIVE: Following Directions and Processes

_____ Assists when feeding
- Needs only a little assistance in getting nipple to mouth
- Uses own hands to guide nipple

_____ Follows adult's cues
- Waves bye-bye when prompted

_____ Continues simple game
- Continues to play a game like pat-a-cake when adult stops playing

_____ Follows simple requests
- The need for adult's approval encourages cooperation ("Please put the dolly in the cradle.")

_____ Follows two-step directions
- Has no trouble with two-step directions ("Please put your crayons in the box and place the box on the shelf")

_____ Imitates multi-step process
- Can follow a multi-step process, such as watercolor painting (dip, paint, wash, tap on sponge) if imitating adult

_____ Remembers multi-step process
- Can follow routine multi-step process such as painting from memory
- Responds to three-part directions

_____ Independent with process
- Dresses self completely
- Manages routines independently
- Still needs directions given in natural order

The young child learns to follow directions in the context of a positive relationship with the adult.

COGNITIVE: Numbers and Counting

This developmental timeline begins around age 1½ in a typically developing child.

_____ Pre-counting
- Fills and empties containers
- Works a simple puzzle where pieces are whole objects

_____ Number words
- Uses a few number words without understanding quantity (imitates a simple counting rhyme)

_____ Beginning counting
- Rote counts to five
- Begins to count objects with one-to-one correspondence[6]
- Understands "many" and "same"

_____ Practicing counting
- Rote counts to ten
- Counts well with one-to-one correspondence
- Understands "tallest," "biggest," "more," and "most"

_____ Recognizes numerals
- Recognizes numerals
- Rote counts to 20+
- Understands "less than"
- Recognizes specific coins

Young children naturally look for opportunities to count things.

COGNITIVE DEVELOPMENT

COGNITIVE: Drawing (Curves and Lines)

The Drawing timelines begin around age 1½ or 2 years (whenever the child begins to draw). Drawing development varies widely, but typically progresses in the developmental manner shown.

_____ Scribbles
- Scribbles do not seem purposeful

_____ Whirling movement
- Child draws a whirl of circles that appear to have no beginning or end
- Lines are drawn with pendulum-like swinging movement

_____ Focal point in center
- Child's circles show a movement that comes to a focal point in the center

_____ Experiences self
- Development of self leads to consciously closing the circle
- Draws straight lines in the form of a cross

_____ Development of self
- Child puts point in the center of the circle
- Extends the cross to become a star

_____ Mandalas
- Child begins to draw two or more shapes with a common center (such as a cross inside a circle)

_____ Suns/radials/squares
- Paths of movement lead from inside outwards, with lines radiating to edge of circle and beyond
- Rectangles and squares appear

_____ Triangle
- The triangle appears in drawings

Swinging movement

Whirling movement

Focal point in center

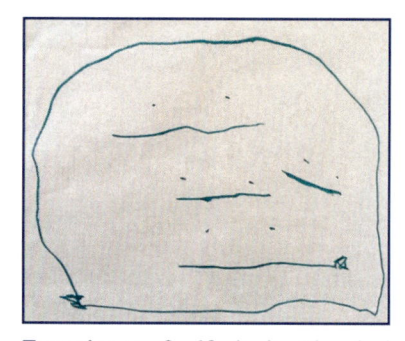

Experience of self: closing the circle

Experience of self: closing the circle 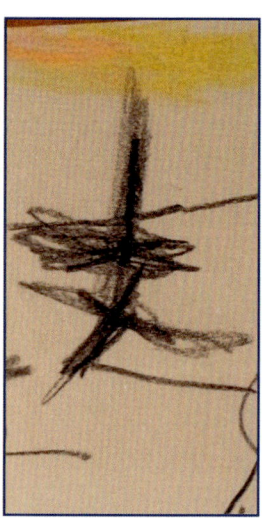   Experience of self: cross

54 OBSERVING YOUNG CHILDREN

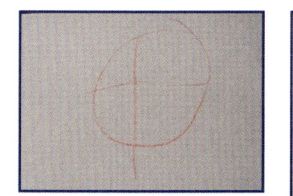

Development of self

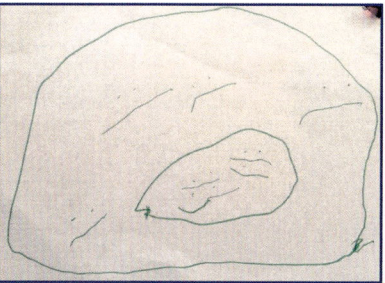

Mandalas

Suns/radials

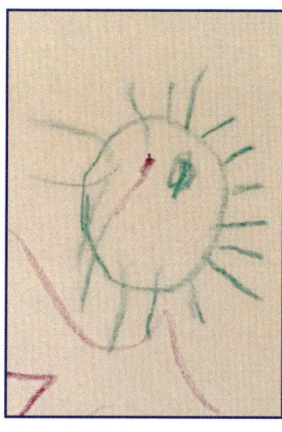

Suns/radials

Rectangles/squares

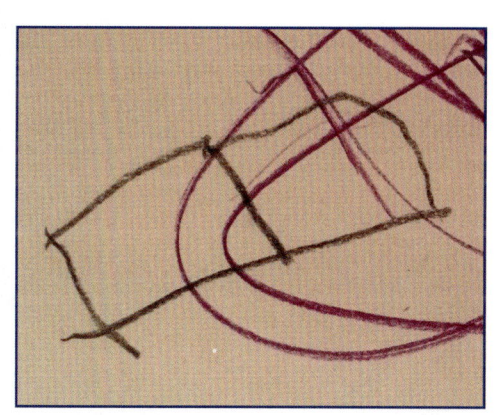

Rectangles/squares

Triangles

Triangles

COGNITIVE DEVELOPMENT **55**

COGNITIVE: Drawing (People and Houses)

The Drawing timelines begin around age 1½ or 2 years (whenever the child begins to draw). Drawing development varies widely, but typically progresses in the developmental manner shown.

_____ Scribbles

- Scribbles do not seem purposeful

_____ Head and trunk

- Pictures of human shape are wholly unconscious
- Drawings consist solely of "head" and "trunk"

_____ Head, trunk and limbs

- Head, trunk and limbs are incorporated into the figure in a symbolic way

_____ Houses

- Human figures are drawn inside "houses" (boxes where the walls fit snugly around the figures inside)

_____ Ladders

- The rib cage arises unconsciously to picture form with "ladders"
- Limbs grow disproportionately long

_____ Head and limb people

- "Head and limb" people arise
- Child may draw them by the dozens and fill whole pages with them

_____ Feet

- True feet appear on human images, standing on the earth
- Pictures of people, houses and trees begin to tell a story

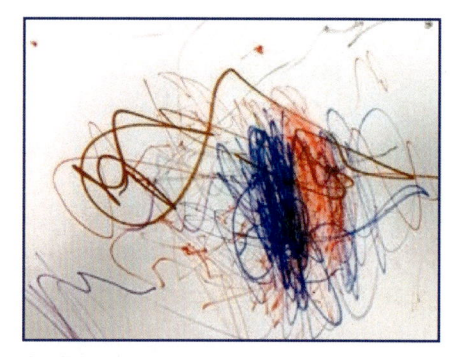

Scribbles

Head and trunk

Head and trunk

Head, trunk and limbs

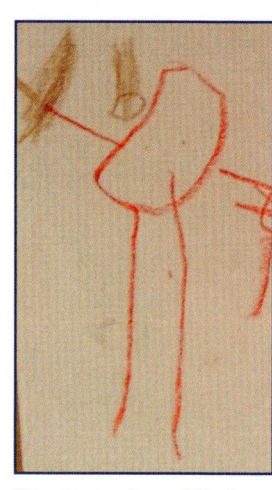

Head, trunk and limbs

56 OBSERVING YOUNG CHILDREN

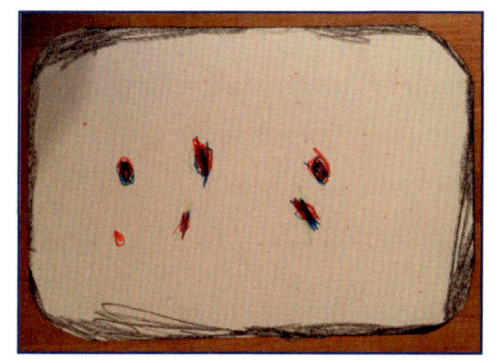

Houses

Houses

Ladders

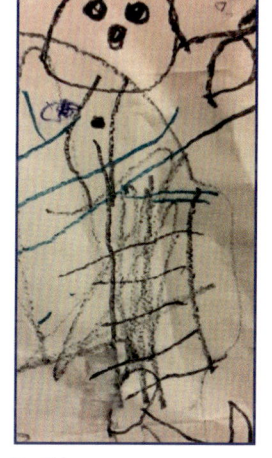

Ladders

Head and limb people

Head and limb people

Feet on ground, roots on trees

COGNITIVE DEVELOPMENT 57

COGNITIVE: Problem-Solving

_____ **Follows objects/people**
- Continues to gaze in the direction of objects/people that have disappeared

_____ **Begins to understand causality**
- Bangs objects to make sounds
- Hands music box or toy back to adult to rewind

_____ **Repetition**
- Increases rate of usual activity with an object when it stops working (e.g., pushes the button repeatedly)

_____ **Imitation**
- Imitates adult action to solve a problem

_____ **Uses tools to solve problems**
- Extends own reach with a stick
- Reaches something high by climbing onto a stool

_____ **Experiments with cause and effect**
- Experiments with cause and effect in play
- Solves problems through trial and error
- Tries different things to solve a problem

_____ **Works with others**
- Likes to work with others to solve a problem
- May become frustrated if a problem cannot be solved quickly

_____ **Creative thinking**
- Thinks about a solution without actually having to try it out
- Enjoys creative thinking, such as suggesting more than one solution to a problem

The preschool-aged child enjoys working with others to solve problems and make things work.

58 OBSERVING YOUNG CHILDREN

LANGUAGE: Non-verbal Communication

_____ Imitates gestures
- Imitates gestures modeled by another (clapping)

_____ Learns simple gestures
- Shakes head for "no"
- Uses simple gestures when asked (e.g., waving bye-bye to someone)

_____ Responds with gestures
- Responds to simple questions with appropriate head movement
- Uses pointing or pulling to direct adult attention

_____ Accompanies words with gestures
- Accompanies simple verbal requests with insistent gesture

_____ Initiates interaction
- Initiates interaction with physical movement (overly affectionate with hugs and kisses, squeezes the cat)

_____ Defensive movement
- May resort to aggressive movement to defend toys and possessions
- May grab, hit with or hide playthings

_____ Verbal and non-verbal aggression
- Relies (most of the time) on verbal rather than physical aggression

_____ Eye contact
- Maintains eye contact when spoken to (unless this is a cultural taboo)

The preschool-aged child begins to learn to communicate without physical aggression.

LANGUAGE DEVELOPMENT

LANGUAGE: Vocabulary and Syntax

| _____ *Mainly vowels*
- Produces a full range of vowels and some consonants

| _____ *Sentence-like babble*
- Babbles in sentence-like sequences
- Produces syllables and sounds with language-like inflection

| _____ *Few words and more gestures*
- Uses gestures such as pulling or pointing to direct adult's attention
- Indicates a few desired objects by name

| _____ *Learning more words*
- Acquires and uses 5–50 words (typically animals, food and toys)

| _____ *Uses the negative*
- Expresses negative statements by tacking on a negative word such as "no" or "not"

| _____ *Expanded noun phrases and plural*
- Uses adjectives and adverbs ("big, brown dog")
- Uses "-s" to indicate more than one (dogs, babies, mouses)

| _____ *Elaborate sentence structure*
- Produces full, elaborate sentences ("The cat ran under the house before I could see what color it was.")

Complex language

- Uses "would" and "could" appropriately
- Uses past tense of verbs (ran, caught, went)
- Adds "-ed" to words to make them past tense

Time spent with a loving adult reading stories builds a rich vocabulary.

LANGUAGE: Conversation

_____ Imitates
- Imitates some non-speech sounds
- Produces full range of vowels
- "Talks" happily to self, toys and people

_____ Babbles
- Babbles and jabbers deliberately to initiate social interaction

_____ Uses jargon
- Produces lots of jargon (puts words and sounds together into speech-like patterns)

_____ Uses phrases
- Produces two-word phrases to express a complete thought ("Want milk")

_____ Understands
- Uses three- to four-word statements
- Understands more language than is able to verbalize
- Much of child's talk has meaning to him/her

_____ Adds to conversation
- Answers simple questions appropriately
- Talks about objects, events and people not present
- Adds information ("Yeah, and then...")

_____ Adapts to listener
- Changes tone of voice and sentence structure to adapt to listener (speaks "baby talk" to baby and sentences to adults)

_____ Complex conversation
- Regularly produces sentences with five to seven or more words

A fully present adult is vital for the child who is learning to converse.

62 OBSERVING YOUNG CHILDREN

LANGUAGE: Expressive Language

_____ Noises
- Makes urgent noises to spur adult into action

_____ First words
- First words (not clear) appear (mama, bye-bye, night-night, dada)

_____ Names objects
- Indicates a few desired objects by name

_____ One- or two-word phrases
- Produces one or two word phrases to express a complete thought ("more" or "want milk")

_____ Describes things
- Draws adult's attention to something by naming it ("elephant") or describing an attribute ("big!")

_____ Asks questions
- Asks increasing questions to obtain information or keep the conversation going

_____ Annoying talk
- May try the adult's patience with silly talk, constant chatter, endless questions, bathroom talk

_____ Functional talk
- Uses functional language when describing things ("A ball is to bounce." "A bed is for sleeping.")
- Describes related concepts ("I got up early when it was still dark.")

Little ones of all ages can practice expressive language when in the company of elders who enjoy children.

LANGUAGE DEVELOPMENT 63

LANGUAGE: Attending to and Comprehending Meaning from Books

This developmental timeline begins around age 6–12 months in a typically developing child.

_____ Responds
- Responds to stories and pictures by vocalizing and patting pictures

_____ Enjoys experience
- Enjoys being held and read to

_____ Enjoys illustrations
- Enjoys looking at picture books

_____ Participates
- Likes to participate in reading (points, names pictures)

_____ Growing attention span
- Will sit and listen to a story from a book for up to ten minutes at a time
- Imitates action of reading a book aloud

_____ Re-tells stories
- Re-tells stories that have been read to him or her

_____ Tells a story
- Tells a familiar story while looking at the pictures in a book
- May read simple books on his or her own

Beautiful picture books help children develop a positive relationship to reading.

LANGUAGE: Listening to and Understanding Oral Stories

This developmental timeline begins around age 3 in a typically developing child.

Repetition

- Loves listening to the same story over and over
- "Rehearses" specific words and lines
- May jump ahead to what happens next in a familiar story

Remembers

- Loves stories about how things grow and how things work
- Remembers parts of a story

Understands and attends

- Can sit still and listen to a short oral story without distraction
- Likes to predict what will happen next

Children's delight in stories helps to build their attention span.

The foundation for lifelong literacy is fostered through storytelling and puppetry.

LANGUAGE DEVELOPMENT

LANGUAGE: Rhyming, Storytelling and Jokes

This developmental timeline begins around age 3 in a typically developing child.

_____ Re-tells stories
- Re-tells a familiar story

_____ Word play
- Boasts, exaggerates and bends the truth with made-up stories
- Delights in word play
- Makes up rhymes

_____ Jokes
- Likes to tell jokes, entertain and make people laugh
- Makes up simple jokes
- Tells simple stories using full sentences

Sharing jokes with friends helps children build language skills.

Playing with language brings delight to the young child.

66 OBSERVING YOUNG CHILDREN

LANGUAGE: Letters, Sounds, Symbols and Writing

This developmental timeline begins around age 3 in a typically developing child.

LifeWays North America does not recommend formal reading instruction for children younger than first grade. The developmental milestones in this section are those that may be achieved by some children independently, without instruction, out of their own natural curiosity, inspired by living in a world of printed works.

_____ Beginning
- Can copy a circle

_____ Special words
- Begins to copy some capital letters
- May be able to print own name
- May recognize printed words that have special meaning

_____ Copies shapes and letters
- Copies a triangle and other shapes
- Can print some letters or numbers
- May name upper and lower case letters

When the child is ready, he will begin to write letters on his own.

LANGUAGE DEVELOPMENT 67

APPROACH TO LEARNING

We may observe factors that affect the way a child approaches learning and responds to life experiences—his or her emerging temperament, learning style and family culture:

1. The Child's Nature: Infants and young children differ in their activity levels, their alertness, and their responses to stimuli. Such differences may lead adults to label children, for example, as an "easy" baby, a "strong-willed" child, a "shy" girl or a "moody" boy. These labels have a definite effect on how people respond to the child, and their responses, in turn, reinforce the child's self-perception. As the young child's temperament is still emerging and somewhat fluid, the temperament types used by Waldorf educators (choleric, sanguine, melancholic and phlegmatic) are more helpful in working with adults and children beyond age six. Still, we can begin to observe the ways in which the young child approaches situations and people without being quick to label him or her.

What have you observed about the nature of this child that may help you to understand how s/he approaches life? *(Examples: The child adjusts easily to new situations, is very active, is easily distracted, is hesitant to join in a new situation until s/he is comfortable, finds transitions challenging, etc.)*

_____

_____

_____

_____

_____
_____
_____
_____
_____
_____
_____
_____
_____
_____

2. Learning Style(s): In general, young children are hands-on, kinesthetic learners. As we get to know a particular child we may notice that other learning styles are present or emerging. Some learning styles we might begin to recognize in the young child are:

> *Hands-on (needs to touch things to learn about them)*
>
> *Bodily/kinesthetic/active (learns through moving the body)*
>
> *Musically inclined*
>
> *Visual/spatial (needs to see something before doing it)*
>
> *Verbal/linguistic (sensitive to language; uses language easily)*
>
> *Interpersonal (learns new skills more quickly when interacting with others)*
>
> *Intrapersonal (prefers to master new skills by him/herself)*

Record any observations you have made about the child's learning style here:

_____
_____
_____
_____
_____

_____
_____
_____
_____
_____
_____
_____

3. *Culture:* **The child's approach to learning is influenced by his/her family, culture and community.**

Record any observations here. (Examples: The child plays best with items that are familiar to those s/he experiences at home; the child is from a dual-language household; the child prefers certain interactions that are similar to those s/he is familiar with, etc.)

_____
_____
_____
_____
_____
_____
_____
_____
_____
_____
_____

CONCLUSION

However you choose to use this guide, I hope it becomes a helpful tool in your observation tool belt. Any practice of observation and assessment that becomes a paperwork drudge taking you away from the children is not helpful! I pray that you can incorporate this tool in your daily life with the children in such a way that it enhances your interactions, helps you learn more about the children in your care, and gives you greater confidence in knowing how to meet their needs. Blessings on your work.

It will indeed come to be for us as a necessity
That we observe the children day by day
And also exercise in ourselves day by day
Control of our own thought and feelings.

Every child has a subtle perception
Of whether the person looking after him
Or teaching him is inwardly equipped in her soul.
The child's well-being depends to a great extent
On what is growing and developing in the inner soul
Of the person in charge.

Develop your keenness of observation;
Nurture the powers of your Inner Being;
Develop vitality of thinking;
Depth of feeling, strength of willing.

—HERBERT HAHN

RESEARCH-BASED TOOLS

The Developmental Timelines have been developed using research-based tools. Data was gathered from the following sources.

Allen, K.E., & Marotz, L.R. (2010). Developmental profiles, pre-birth through twelve. Clifton Park, NY: Thomson/Delmar Learning.

Johnson-Martin, Nancy; Attermeier, Susan & Hacker, Bonnie (1990). The Carolina curriculum for preschoolers with special needs. Baltimore, MD: Paul H. Brookes Publishing Co.

Johnson-Martin, Nancy; Jens, Kenneth; Attermeier, Susan & Hacker, Bonnie (1991). The Carolina curriculum for infants and toddlers with special needs (Second Edition). Baltimore, MD: Paul H. Brookes Publishing Co.

Smith, Charles A., PhD (October 1999). At the Heart of Their Art, Kansas State University Agricultural Experiment Station and Cooperative Extension Service Fact Sheet.

Strauss, Michaela (2007). Understanding children's drawings, tracing the path of incarnation. Forest Row, UK: Rudolf Steiner Press.

Other Resources

Aldinger, Cynthia (2015). Life is the curriculum: exploring the foundations of care for young children through the insights of Rudolf Steiner, founder of Waldorf education. Norman, OK: LifeWays North America.

Selg, Peter (2008). The therapeutic eye: How Rudolf Steiner observed children. Great Barrington, MA: SteinerBooks.

Clark, Laurie (Fall/Winter 2009). A Contemplative and Reflective Format for Early Childhood Study, Gateways. Spring Valley, NY: Waldorf Early Childhood Association of North America (WECAN).

Florez, Ida Rose (July 2011). Developing Young Children's Self-Regulation through Everyday Experiences, Young children. Washington, DC: National Association for the Education of Young Children.

LifeWays North America (2015). Integration of Learning Requirements for LifeWays Early Childhood Certificate Students.

Poole, Carla; Miller, Susan A. & Booth Church, Ellen (2013). Ages and Stages: All About Body Awareness, early childhood today. New York: Scholastic, Inc. .

_____. (January 2000). Ages and Stages: Learning to Follow Directions, Scholastic early childhood today. New York: Scholastic, Inc.

_____. (2013). Problem-solving in Action, Scholastic early childhood today. New York: Scholastic: Inc.

Wisconsin Model Early Learning Standards (WMELS), Wisconsin Dept. of Public Instruction.

ENDNOTES

1. Self-regulation refers to complicated processes that allow children to respond appropriately to their environment. Children must learn to evaluate what they take in with their senses and communicate with bodily systems (such as motor or language systems) to choose and carry out a response.

2. Beyond the types of play listed on the developmental continuum, it is important to also observe and note the following necessary types of play which do not fit neatly on a timeline:
   - Dramatic/fantasy play – Role playing, dressing up
   - Competitive play – "Let's both jump off this log and see who can jump the farthest!"
   - Physical play – Less about being social (although it can be social) and more about being physical. Roughhousing falls into this category. Often adults see this as a problem, but it is vital to development.
   - Constructive play – Building, fitting things together, taking things apart.

3. The Moro reflex, also known as the startle reflex, is an involuntary response that is present at birth and usually disappears between the ages of three to six months. The reflex occurs when an infant is startled by a loud noise or other environmental stimulus or feels that he or she is falling and causes the baby to extend the arms, legs and fingers and arch the back.

4. Please note, young children are "do-ers," not "sitters!" They can come to stillness at meals, story time or nap time only if they have been allowed plenty of movement and time in the fresh air.

5. Rudolf Steiner, founder of Waldorf education, described twelve senses actively at work in the human being. Modern researchers have identi-

fied as many as 21. Steiner's primary four senses of Touch, Life, Self-movement and Balance are central to the development of the young child. These four senses are represented throughout these developmental timelines. The senses focused on in the developmental timeline titled "Senses" are the traditional five most of us were taught in grade school: Sight, Hearing, Taste, Smell and Touch.

6. "One to one correspondence" means matching one object with another object. Setting the table, matching one plate with each chair, is a good example. Counting with one-to-one correspondence means matching a number to an object as the child counts them, "One, two, three, four, etc." while pointing to the next object. In the beginning, children often skip objects as they do this.

Made in the USA
Middletown, DE
30 March 2019